DIRTY DITTIES

Collected by
Michael Rosen

Illustrated by
Riana Duncan

André Deutsch

First published in 1990 by
André Deutsch Limited
105-106 Great Russell Street, London WC1B 3LJ

Second impression 1990
Third impression August 1991
Fourth impression November 1991
Fifth impression February 1992

British Library Cataloguing in Publication Data
Dirty ditties.
   1. Poetry in English. Anthologies
   1. Rosen, Michael
   821.008

ISBN 0 233 98619 7

Printed in Great Britain by
WBC Limited, Bridgend

Foreword

In 1989, we published the first ever book of the kind of rude rhymes written by no one knows who and passed on by word of mouth. It was a great success and sold out in weeks. In the foreword to *Rude Rhymes*, I suggested that readers might like to contribute to Volume II. I wondered, are there more rhymes out there? Well, there are. Stacks of them and they've been flooding in; a girl in Cumbria, a couple from Australia, Mother-in-law (not mine) in London, police in Ealing and so on. Some people were proud enough of their memories to want to see their names after the rhyme. I was intrigued that a 'Godliman' and an 'Angel' were amongst them, and that girls from such respectable places as Surrey, Kent, Buckinghamshire and Hampstead were keen to contribute.

Last time, various complaints were made:

Surely they weren't all really childhood rhymes?
Yes, they were but this time there's no age limit.

Surely I was censoring some rhymes?
Yes I was and am again. I like to be discerning about my smut.

Surely this whole thing is an absurd enterprise?
It has always seemed strange to me that though millions of people enjoy hearing fantastic rhymes about what our bodies can or might do, none of this was written down where we could all read it. Why should we be restricted to just the ones friends and relations had told us, I asked

myself. Wasn't this the sort of thing the printing press was invented for?

Surely something needed to be said about the rhymes? Of course, I could gas on about the role of the fart or the symbolism of squashed balls but it would set people yawning not laughing.

So thanks to all of you who wrote in – who knows, there might be yet more out there for a volume III. Send them in by the sackload to Michael Rosen, c/o André Deutsch Ltd, 105–106, Great Russell Street, London WC1B 3LJ. Please give details of from whom, how old (or young) and where. Your reward will be a free copy and, if you're willing to own up to it, an acknowledgement.

DIRTY
DITTIES

Spider, spider
on the wall,
ain't you got no
sense at all?
Can't you see
the wall's been plastered?
Now you're stuck
you silly bastard.

Karen Godliman, 13
Woking, Surrey

A fairy's life is very hard,
up where the tinsel flickers.
Golden wand in one hand,
and a fir tree up her knickers.

Karen Godliman, 13
Woking, Surrey

Goosey Goosey Gander
where do you wander?
Upstairs and downstairs
and in my lady's chamber.
There I saw an old man
playing with his dick.
So I took him by the left leg
and gave his arse a kick.

policeman, 40
Ealing, Middlesex

Sung

Good King Wenceslas looked out
upon his cabbage garden.
He farted on a brussels sprout
and said, I beg your pardon.

girl, 8
Surrey

'Tis a man's occupation
to stick his knobulation
up a woman's ventilation
to increase the population
of the younger generation.
I got this information
from the board of education
after a detailed demonstration
by two teachers on the floor.

Karen Godliman, 13
Woking, Surrey

A potato is a potato
a tomato is a tomato
and a pea is a relief.

Karen Godliman, 13
Woking, Surrey

Jack and Jill went up the hill
to do some hanky-panky.
Jack went, 'Ooh,'
Jill went, 'Ahh,'
then out popped Baby Frankie.

Karen Godliman, 13
Woking, Surrey

Jack and Jill went to the dairy
Jack pulled out his big and hairy.
Jill said, 'Oh what a whopper,
let's get down and do it proper.'

girl, 11, London, Richard Griffiths, 25, Beeston, Notts,
Jamie Jones, 12, Manchester, Mark Poole, 15, East Yorkshire

Old Mother Hubbard
went to the cupboard
to fetch poor Rover a bone
when she bent over
Rover took over
and gave her a bone of his own.

Reg Palmer, 20, Middlesex,
Richard Dod, 13, S. Wirral

Tune: 'My Bonnie Lies Over The Ocean'

My daddy lies over the ocean
my mummy lies over the sea.
My daddy laid over my mummy
and that's how they got little me.

children, 10
Kensington, London

Georgie Porgie pudding and pie
kissed the girls and made them cry.
When the boys came out to play
he kissed them too – he's funny that way.

Georgie (!), 5
Hammersmith

Tune: 'D'ye ken John Peel?'

Oh-h cats on the rooftops, cats on the tiles
cats with the clap and cats with piles
cats with their arseholes wreathed in smiles,
as they revel in the joys of fornication.

Bill, 36
Ealing

Mary had a little lamb . . .
. . . she got 2 years for perverting a minor
and 10 for bestiality.

boy, 17
near Godalming

Mary had a little lamb
it was as white as snow.
She put it on the mantlepiece
and it piddled in granma's cocoa.

Kerry Connor, 11
Sennelager, Germany

Mary had a little watch
she used it as a garter
when the boys asked the time
she knew what they were after.

Danny, 36
Bromley, Kent

Mary had a little lamb,
she tied it to a pylon.
10,000 volts went up its arse,
and turned its wool to nylon.

Lee Dawson Geldard, 14, Bridlington, North Humberside,
Karen Godliman, 13, Woking, Surrey, Jamie Jones, 12, Manchester,
Eileen McLarnon, 14, Lincs

Mary had a little sheep
With her one night, it went to sleep.
The sheep turned out to be a ram,
now Mary has a little lamb.

playground (4 year olds), Hammersmith,
1989

Mary had a little lamb
she kept it as a pet.
And when the price of meat went up,
she ate the little get.

Mary had a little lamb
she fed it on crackers.
Every time it jumped the fence
it landed on its knackers.

Lee Dawson Geldard, 14
Bridlington, North Humberside

Mary had a little lamb
the butcher chopped it dead,
she took it to school the next day
between two hunks of bread.

John Bolt,
Stroud, Gloucs

Mary had a little lamb
she kept it in a bucket
and everytime the lamb jumped out,
the bulldog tried to put it back again.

John Bolt,
Stroud, Gloucs

Mary had a little lamb
the doctor was surprised
but when Macdonald had a farm
he couldn't believe his eyes.

Richard Griffiths, 25
Beeston, Notts

Little Robin Redbreast
sat upon a pole,
lifted up his left leg
and whistled up his hole.

Danny, 36
Bromley, Kent

Silence in court,
The judge is dead.
Someone has farted
and blew off his head.

Kerry Connor, 11
Sennelager, Germany

Julius Caesar, dropped a breezer,
his mother went to catch it.
His father hid behind the door
and hit it with a hatchet.

K. Da'Casto, 19
Newbury, Berks

Tune: 'Rule Britannia'

Rule Britannia
two tanners make a bob.
Good King Henry
never shaved his knob.

Richard Griffiths, 25
Beeston, Notts

Tune: 'Red Flag'

The working class can kiss my arse
I've got the foreman's job at last.
If you're out of work and on the dole,
you can stick the Red Flag up your hole.

John Bolt,
Stroud, Gloucs

In days of old
when knights were bold
and condoms weren't invented
they wrapped their socks
around their cocks
and babies were prevented.

Lee Dawson Geldard, 14
Bridlington, North Humberside

In days of old when knights were bold
and toilets weren't invented,
they dropped their load
in the middle of the road
and went home quite contented.

woman, 50
Holland

In days of old
when knights were bold
and woman weren't invented
they drilled some holes
in telegraph poles
and had to be contented.

Gary Welsh, 24
Bristol

Poor old Santa, poor old guy,
by jeepers and by jiminy,
he only comes but once a year
and then it's down the chiminey.

man, first heard in 1962
USA

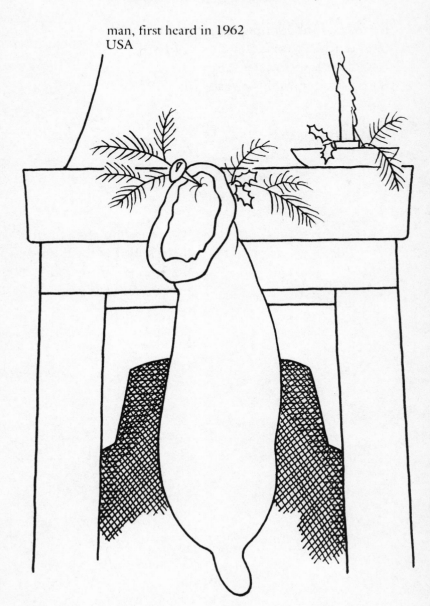

There was Superman flying around
when he spotted Supergirl lying on the ground.
In the nude, legs in air, he thought, 'What luck!
I'll nip down quick and give her a fuck!'

Batman grabbed him as he flew past:
'You're much too late, you stupid arse.
You'd get a shock,' he said with a grin.
'The Invisible Man's already in.'

Frank, 43
Brentford, Middx

'Who do you stick up for?'
'I stick up for my mum.'
'I stick up for my dad
he stuck up for me.'

man, 60
Middlesex

What's the time? Half past nine
hang your knickers on the line.
When they're dry, bring them in,
put them in a biscuit tin.
Eat a biscuit, eat a cake,
eat your knickers by mistake.

girl, 8
Surrey

There was a young man from St Paul's
who possessed the most useless of balls.
One night in the Strand
he managed to stand
and tossed himself off in the stalls.

Lee Dawson Geldard, 14
Bridlington, North Humberside

There was a young actress from Kew
who said, as the bishop withdrew,
'The vicar is quicker,
and slicker and thicker,
and three inches longer than you.'

Michael Sharp Jnr, 16
Leeds

There was a young fellow from Brent
whose knob was unusually bent.
So to save him the trouble,
he put it in double
and instead of coming, he went.

man, 46
London

There was a young plumber named Lee
who plumbed his girl down by the sea.
Said the lady, 'Stop plumbing,
I hear someone coming.'
Said the plumber, still plumbing, 'That's me!'

Carla Holden, 15
Cumbria

There was an old man from Boshum
who took out his balls to wash 'em.
Then his wife said, 'Jack,
if you don't put 'em back
I will stamp on the fuckers and squash 'em.'

Eileen McLarnon, 14, Grantham, Lincs, girl, 11, London

The boy stood on the burning deck,
his lips were all a-quiver.
He gave a cough
and his cock fell off
and floated down the river.

Kate Lawrie, 18, and sister, 19, Bucks

The boy stood on the burning deck
with a pocketful of crackers,
the flames shot up his trouser leg
and blew off both his knackers.

Paul Stanfield, 22
Stoke-on-Trent

The boy stood on the burning deck
the flames around him flickers.
He said, 'It doesn't bother me,
I've got asbestos knickers.'

Sheila, 17
Hampstead, London

There was a young woman called Ransom
who was fucked nine times in a Hansom.
When she called out for more,
the man on the floor
said, 'My name's Simpson, not Samson.'

man, 46
London

The first mate's name was Carter
and boy! was he a farter
when the wind was low
and the ship wouldn't go
they used Carter the Farter to start'er.

John, 28, and Linda, 25, Motyka
Melbourne, Australia

There was a young man called Perkins
who took a fond liking to gherkins.
One day on a spree
he ate two-forty-three
and fucked up his internal workings.

Nick the Greek, 26
London

Chant:

'Balls to the baker.'
'BROWN BREAD!'

'Who fucked the baker?'
'OLD FRED!'

'Where did he do it?'
'IN BED!'

'What were his balls like?'
'ALL RED!'

'How do you know that?'
'I'M FRED!'

Nick the Greek, 26
London

Mistress Mary,
quite contrary,
how hairy
is your canary?
Three or four
inches long?
Or are you a toff
and shave them off?

Nick the Greek, 26
London

Tune: 'Daisy Daisy'

Daisy, Daisy,
give me your tits to chew.
I'm half crazy
my bollocks are turning blue.
I can't afford a durex
a plastic bag will do.
but you'll look sweet
upon the seat,
with me on top of you.

Kate Angel, 21, London,
(slightly different version) Julian Foster, 18, Beckenham, Kent

Tune: 'Jailhouse Rock'

I went to a party down the county jail
I caught my cock on a rusty nail.
When I got home I was in for a shock:
I only had one ball on my cock.

I've been invited to a nudist colony,
I won't go, oh deary, deary me
because they'll be laughing at my dapper
saying I look like Adolf Hitler.

Nick the Greek, 26
London

Tune: 'Puff the Magic Dragon'

Puff the magic dragon,
pissed in the sea
so they rubbed his bum
in boiling rum
for doing this, you see.

man, 32
Johannesburg, South Africa

It was Christmas day in the workhouse
the mould was on the walls,
the vicar was preaching to the inmates
and someone shouted, 'Balls!'

'I'll give you balls, you bastard,
you damned ungrateful sod,
I'll stop your Christmas pudding,
I'll see to that, by God.'

All was silent when Michael Rosen [or whoever]
shouted out, as bold as brass,
'We don't want your Christmas pudding,
you can stuff it up your arse.'

'Seize him,' shouted the vicar,
himself he found hard to restrain.
On this Holy order, Rosen's head went down the lavatory
pan,
and some cunt pulled the chain.

John Bolt,
Stroud, Gloucs

Arsehole,
arsehole,
a soldier I shall be,
to piss,
to piss,
two pistols on my knee,
fuck you,
fuck you,
for curiosity,
I'll fight for the old cunt
fight for the old cunt,
fight for the old country.

Richard Griffiths, 25, Beeston, Notts,
girl, 12, Cambridgeshire

The fart is a wonderful creature
it lives in the Valley of Bum.
It travels around in your knickers
and comes out with a musical hum.

Kate Angel, 21
London

Tune: Regimental March of the Grenadier Guards

There was a Scots Highlander
at the Battle of Waterloo,
a wind blew up his tartan kilt
and showed his cock-a-doodle-do.
He thought it was so pretty,
he showed it to the queen.
She said, 'Don't be so dirty,
and go and wash it clean.'

woman, 46
London

Tune: Cub Scouts' Song 'Woodpecker's Hole

Oh I put my finger up a woodpecker's hole
the woodpecker said, 'God bless my soul!
keep it up
keep it up
keep it up
gor blimey.

I stuck it up once, I stuck it up twice
the woodpecker said, 'Oh Christ, that's nice
keep it up
keep it up
keep it up
gor blimey.

man, 46, and mother-in-law,
London

Tune: 'I've been everywhere, man'

I was sitting in the corner
of a dirty greasy spoon cafe.
I was putting on the relish
when the man beside me came to say,
'What's that pubic hair doin'
sittin' layin' on yer bins?'
I said I didn't see it there,
could it really be the one?
He jumped upon the counter
and he said, 'Hey looky here
ah bin all over the country
an' ah seen pubic hair.

Ah seen pubic hair, man
more than ah kin bear, man,
even got my share, man
beneath mah underwear, man
ah seen pubic hair, man.'

Sheila, 17
Hampstead, London

'My daughter will now sing.'
'Will she, fuck!'
'One question at a time, please.'

man, 60
Middlesex

Here lies the body
of dear old Dick
who went through life
with a twisted prick.

All his life
was a lifelong hunt
looking for the girl
with the twisted cunt.

When he found one
he dropped down dead,
for the one he found
had a left hand thread.

man, 70
London

Tune: 'Colonel Bogey'

Hitler
has only got one ball
Goering
has two but very small
Himmler
is very sim'lar
and poor old Goebbels
has no balls at all.

man, 43
Middlesex

It depends how you read it:

BRITISH TROOPS' PUSH
Bottles up Germans
(newspaper headline: 1944)

or

BRITISH TROOPS
PUSH BOTTLES UP GERMANS

Who is Sylvia? What is she?
(Elizabethan song)

or

Who is Sylvia?
What?
Is she?

man, 40-ish
Reading, Berks

Headline in US paper:

NUT SCREWS WASHER AND BOLTS

man, 43
Middx

Now here's a simple story
as simple as can be.
The place is Piccadilly,
the players: He and She.

She says, 'Will it hurt me?'
'Of course not,' says he.
'Its just a simple process,
as simple as can be.'

He gives a sudden jerk,
she cries, 'It bloody hurts,
thank God it's all over,
thank God he's pulled it out.'

Now, if you read this carefully,
a Dentist you will find.
It's not what you were thinking,
it's just your dirty mind.

Julie Harrison, 20
Swansea, Wales

What are three bad things about being a dick?
1. Your two best mates are nuts and an arsehole.
2. Your master covers you with a plastic bag.
3. Every time you get excited, you throw up.

Jack Staples, 13
South London

Tune: 'Captain Pugwash'

Do your balls hang low?
Can you swing 'em to and fro?
Can you tie 'em in a knot?
Can you tie 'em in a bow?
Do you get a funny feeling
when your bollocks hit the ceiling?
Oh you'll never be a sailor
if your balls hang low.

Miss G.K. Crawford
Lincoln

Oh the Grand Old Duke of York
he had ten thousand men.
(And his court case comes up tomorrow.)

Paul Stanfield, 22
Stoke-on-Trent

Good morning, sergeant major
and bless your very soul
I tried to fuck your daughter
but I couldn't find the hole.

When I found the hole
beneath her frilly frock,
believe me, sergeant major
I couldn't find my cock.

When I found my cock
all slimy and thin,
believe me, sergeant major
I couldn't get it in.

When I got it in
and wriggling it all about
believe me, sergeant major
I couldn't get it out.

When I got it out
all red and sore
believe me, sergeant major
the bugger asked for more.

Nick the Greek, 26
London

I saw a young sailor who was sitting on a rock
was swinging and swaying his big hairy . . .

Fist, and the lady next door in the Ritz
was teaching the children to play with her . . .

Ice-creams and marbles and all things galore
along came a lady that looked like . . .

Shakespeare, and he was a man of wit
and on his shirt he had some . . .

Buttons, and while he was passing by St Pauls
a lady came up and grabbed him by the . . .

Arm, and she said you look like a man of pluck,
let's go home and have a cup of tea.

Nick the Greek, 26
London

Tongue-twister

Suzy sits in the shoe-shine shop
she sits and shines
she shines and sits.

Kate Lawrie, 18, and sister, 19, Bucks

The cat crept into the crypt
crapped
and crept out again.

man, 43
London

Say quickly:

I chased a bug around a tree
I'll get his blood he knows I will.

Julian Foster, 18
Beckenham, Kent

When things go wrong
and they usually will
and your daily road
seems all uphill
when machines are down
and tempers high
when you try to smile
but can only cry
and you really feel
you'd like to quit,
don't run to me,
I don't give a shit.

Tim Isaacs, 14
Cambridge

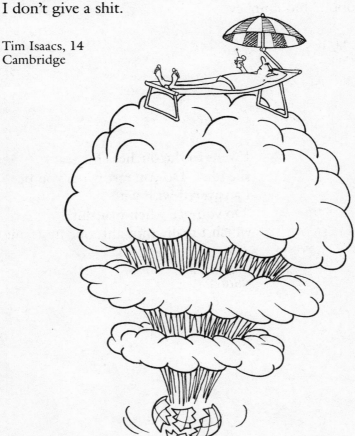

Your Bob
owes our Bob
one bob
and if your Bob
don't give our Bob
that bob
that your Bob
owes our Bob
then our Bob
will give
your Bob
a bobbin' bloomin' eye.

boy, 11
London

I went to the duchess for tea,
she said, 'Do you fart when you pee?'
I answered with wit,
'Do you pee when you shit?'
which I really thought, one up to me.

woman, 73
Norfolk

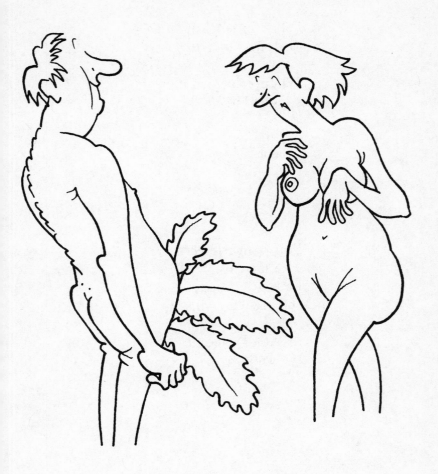

Stiff and straight
long and thin
all wrapped up
in a shiny pink skin.

What is it?

Rhubarb

man, 43
Middlesex

Whoever smelt it
dealt it.

Whoever denied it
supplied it.

boy, 9
London

You want triplets
I want twins.
Let's go to bed
and see who wins.

Ghisleine Quinn, 15
Stockport

My old man's a dustman
he wears a dustman's hat.
He farted through the keyhole
and paralysed the cat.
The chairs couldn't take it,
the table split in half
that's when my dad
done a supersonic fart.

girl, 11
London

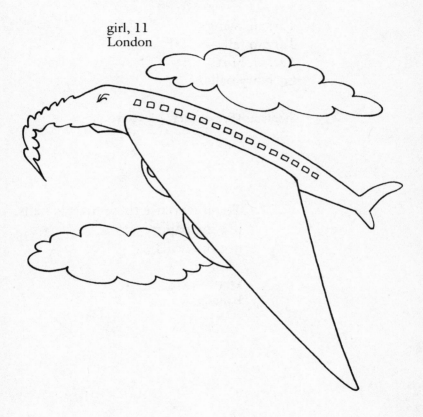

Apple tart makes you fart
custard powder makes it louder.

Michelle Ricketts, 10
Gwent, Wales

Tarzan swings
Tarzan falls
Tarzan hurts
his hairy balls.

Siobhan, 15, and Sara, 16, Herts

To all who use these marble halls,
use the paper
not the walls.

Mother-in-law,
London

Wherever you are
wherever you be
always let
your wind go free
for refraining to fart
was the death of me.

Mother-in-law,
London

WORDS OF WISDOM

When you get them by the balls, their hearts and minds will follow
Good girls go to heaven, bad girls go everywhere
If you miss your period now, don't worry, better late than never
It's the little things that show they care – but yours is too small
Don't leave home without it – your stretchable friend
Make it easy – practise with your pencil case

Siobhan, 15, and Sara, 16, Herts

Roses are red
dahlias are pink
my feet are pretty
but your feet stink.

girl, 12
London

He took me to the pictures
to get me dolly mixtures
and every time the light went out
he looked right up my knickers.

girl, 12
London

A MAN'S LIFE

20–30 Tri-weekly
30–40 Try weekly
40–50 Try weakly
50–60 Beer is best

Nick the Greek, 26
London

Pick it
lick it
roll it
flick it

man, 43
Middlesex

Once a king
always a king
once a knight
is enough.

John, 28, and Linda, 25, Motyka
Melbourne, Australia

Three men were walking along when they came to a cave. One of them went in and saw a piece of toast in there. He went to pick it up when he heard this voice say:

I'M THE GHOST
THAT GUARDS THE TOAST

so the man ran out, and he says to the others,
'Don't go in there, there's a ghost in there.'
But the second man says, 'I ain't scared, I'm going in.'

So he goes in and he sees the piece of toast and he goes to pick it up when he hears the voice:

I'M THE GHOST
THAT GUARDS THE TOAST

so the man ran out and he says to the third man,
'Don't go in there, there's a ghost in there.'
But the third man says, 'I ain't scared, I'm going in.'

So he goes in and he sees the piece of toast and he thinks, I ain't bothered, and he grabbed it and stuffed it in his mouth and ate it all up. And the voice called out:

I WARNED YOU ONCE
I WARNED YOU TWICE
I WIPE MY BUM
ON EVERY SLICE.

boy, 9
London

If all the boys lived over the sea
what a great swimmer, Mary would be.

If all the boys ate greasy chips
wouldn't Mary have greasy lips?

Kate Lawrie, 18, and sister, 19, Bucks

When roses are red
they're ready for plucking
when girls are sixteen
they're ready for fucking.

boy, 10
London

DIRTY BOOK

Run to the Toilet by Willie Makeit

John, 28, and Linda, 25, Motyka
Melbourne, Australia

Spell PIG backwards and add 'funny' to it.

John, 28, and Linda, 25, Motyka
Melbourne, Australia

Try this:

Put your fingers in the corners of your mouth,
pull out your cheeks and say, 'My dad's a banker'.

boy, 13
London